PLYMOUTH'S GOLDEN AGE OF TRAMS

Arthur L. Clamp

GOODBYE TO PLYMOUTH TRAMS

A transport era comes to an end with this beflagged car making the last tram journey in the city on 29th September, 1945. Ths final car left Old Town Street for the Milehouse depot via Peverell Park Road.

This version of the book is virtually as originally published.
There are now additional pages at the back providing information about the author.

The republishing project is being managed by Arthur's grandson, Steven Gibson. We aim to find all the research that he was involved in publishing, preserving it for the next generation as part of 'The Clamp Collection'.

THE TRAMS OF PLYMOUTH

It is hoped that this illustrated booklet will serve as a reminder of the not too distant days when the streets, roads and avenues of the Three Towns resounded with the clanging of tram bells and the metallic rumbling of an approaching tram at what would now seem to be a very slow pace.

Trams were part of the transport fabric of Plymouth, as well as many other large provincial towns, from the early 1880s to 1945. It was the war which brought the death knell of these favourite cars although by the late 1930s other forms of transport of a more flexible nature were usurping the premier position tram cars had in the first three decades of this century.

This booklet is not planned as a compendium of facts and figures about the actual numbers of cars that criss-crossed Plymouth, or the numerous routes used to carry thousands of passengers in and around the area. There are other books and magazines which will supply this kind of information for the "buff". This title is planned to jolt the memory of people who used the trams to get to and from work, for school children who used them to reach school and for families who took a tram ride either to the Hoe or to Little Ash Tea Gardens at St. Budeaux for an afternoon's outing. The many illustrations should also give post-war generations a reasonable idea of how their parents and grandparents moved about before the motor car reached popularity.

The introduction and development of a tramway system in this area was largely influenced by the independence of the three towns of Plymouth, Stonehouse and Devonport who, more or less, pursued their own plans for laying tramlines before the amalgamation of 1914. The companies then eventually came together to serve the whole area based at the large Milehouse depot.

The different companies working in the area were:
Plymouth, Stonehouse and Devonport Tramways Company, 1870.
Plymouth Tramways Company, 1880
Plymouth, Devonport and District Tramway Company, 1884.

They originally worked very short journeys of track within a limited area of the Three Towns and one or other company was reluctant to co-operate and extend their routes. However, with the onset of the First World War, decisions were taken which brought them under one umbrella and by about 1920 trams were moving right across the large town.

Pairs of horses were used for pulling the first trams and they were in use up until 1907. In 1901 there were 47 horse cars and 127 horses serving the public although by this time the much larger electric tram was beginning to replace the horse tram.

This came into service in the middle of the 1890s and soon many routes had the familiar overhead wires which carried the current around the town to power the trams. Cars were either bought from other companies, imported or made at Milehouse. The early electric tram could carry about 42 passengers. The 1920s was the period of greatest investment in rolling stock and maintenance facilities. More robust cars, still with open tops, replaced the first electric trams and these remained in use until the closure of the system during the 1940s.

It was during the 1930s that private motor cars and public buses began to take away passengers and cause traffic problems with the rigid tram which could only travel along a given track route. The same changes in traffic patterns appeared in other places and by the outbreak of the Second World War in 1939, the days of the tram as an effective means of carrying passengers over the expanding city were numbered.

The severe blitz did not spare trams or tracks. Great havoc was caused to the overhead wires, trams were put out of use and the large depot at Milehouse received considerable damage. The ending of hostilities heralded the ending of Plymouth's trams. The system had kept up some sort of service to the public during the war years but could not match the impact more mobile buses were having on moving people around.

Arthur L. Clamp,
203 Elburton Road,
Plymouth, Devon.

Little Ash Gardens,
SALTASH PASSAGE,

("Devonport's Beauty Spot") re-open for the season early in **APRIL**.

Beautiful Grounds, Large Meadow, Swings, Roundabout, See-Saws, Etc.

The ideal place for **Sunday School Outings.**

AMPLE ACCOMMODATION FOR SMALL OR LARGE PARTIES.

HIGH-CLASS TEAS AND REFRESHMENTS AT POPULAR PRICES

Frequent Cars from Stuart Road, Morice Square and Tor Lane. Return Fare, 5d. ; Children, 3d.

For Tea Tariff, Special Cars, & all Particulars:
Apply to THE MANAGER,
Devonport & District Tramways Co.,
Milehouse, Devonport.

N.B.—These GARDENS were visited last Summer by nearly **20,000** *persons.*

LORRY AND TRAMCAR.

ALARMING ACCIDENT AT DEVONPORT.

About 20 persons, a tramcar, and a motor lorry were concerned in an alarming accident at Devonport yesterday, but fortunately no one was seriously injured. The motor lorry, with a three-ton load of vegetables, came out of a side street and proceeded down the hill at Avondale-terrace, followed by a tramcar. About half-way down the hill the tram crashed into the rear of the lorry, and so terrific was the impact that the lorry was turned round completely and toppled over on to its off side. Sacks of cabbages and potatoes were scattered over the road and pavement, and T. Hall, who was riding on the top of the load, was thrown headlong. He escaped with a shaking and an injured ankle. The passengers on the tramcar, although greatly alarmed, were uninjured.

The only material damage to the lorry was a broken steering gear, but the force of the impact completely smashed four of the large panes of glass in the tramcar in addition to damaging the front of the body and the controls. The lorry was subsequently righted and the tram service was soon normal.

"PENNY HITCH" HILL

Tavistock Road was dubbed this title around the turn of this century when horse-drawn trams worked this route. The two normal pulling horses are helped with an extra horse in front while another appears to be walking alongside perhaps returning to the stables which were then on the site of the old Belgrave Cinema on Mutley Plain. Horse-drawn trams were replaced by electric ones on this route in 1905.

GREEN AND WHITE LIVERY OF HORSE-DRAWN CAR

These were the colours of the very early horse-drawn trams which took passengers from the Theatre to Devonport via Union Street and to Mutley Plain via Houndiscombe Road. They date from the commencement of trams in Plymouth during the 1880s and ran until about 1907. This photograph is dated about 1889 and the tram is making its way to the Theatre. The more direct route to Mutley up Tavistock Road was not opened until 1895.

PLYMOUTH, STONEHOUSE AND DEVONPORT HORSE TRAM

This crowded tram is about to enter the Battery Street loop outside the Grand Theatre around 1900 and belonged to the first local company to run trams in the Plymouth area. The original fleet of cars was made up of 8 open toppers, each pulled by a pair of horses, which were stabled in Manor Lane off Manor Street. The route ran from Derry's Clock in Plymouth to Cumberland Gardens, Devonport, via Stonehouse.

THOSE FAR OFF DAYS!

This early picture, taken about 1895, shows one of the Plymouth, Stonehouse and Devonport Company's horse-drawn trams about to enter the crossing loop at the Octagon. This company was the first to operate trams in this area and started taking passengers in March 1872, along a route of 1 mile, 74 chains from the old Clock Tower, Plymouth, to Cumberland Road, Devonport. Two horses pulled the tram assisted by a third when going up Devonport Hill!

A CAREFUL DESCENT OF TAVISTOCK ROAD

This partly damaged photograph dates from the First World War and the tram is coming in from Compton for the Theatre stop. This route was electrified in 1905 and the tram was in service from 1903 to 1934. Cars were not confined to one route. They were moved around as passenger demand changed over the years. Sherwell Church and Queen Anne's Terrace have hardly changed from these days.

TURNING INTO OLD TOWN STREET

The crowded open upper deck of this tram, no. 18, suggests that it is a fine day with no rain about and, from the style of the clothes worn, at the start or end of a working day. This car was introduced into service in 1900 and was withdrawn by 1924. The rear stairs and braking handle can be clearly seen.

GUILDHALL TO WEST HOE SERVICE

This horse-drawn car waits for passengers at West Hoe on a short route which was mainly popular during the summer months. Car no. 1 was in use from 1885 to 1892 and was kept with others in sheds at West Hoe Road together with stables for the horses.

PLYMOUTH CORPORATION TRAMWAY'S DEMI-CAR

Six of these were introduced in 1907, nos. 37 to 42, when the horse-drawn West Hoe route was electrified. They were one-man operated, single decked, and worked from the Theatre to West Hoe and Piers along an extended route facing the Sound. The demi-cars were withdrawn by 1924.

PLYMOUTH'S FIRST ELECTRIC TRAM

This was the first of six new trams introduced in 1899 which were operated until 1924 by the Plymouth Corporation Tramway Company. It is seen here at the Milehouse depot on special duties probably arriving for a service. These trams could each carry 42 passengers and were operated with Westinghouse electrical equipment and were built by Brush on Peckham tracks. Their introduction was marked by them being beflagged on the initial drive to the old Prince Rock depot.

P.C.T. CAR NO. 30 AT MILEHOUSE

Ready for another period of work, this early tram has just been serviced at Milehouse. It was in use from 1903 until 1924 and was one of sixteen new cars introduced to cope with the new routes being developed in the area. The old horse trams were being sold at this period, eleven of which fetched £3. 15. 0d. each! There was then a tram depot at Prince Rock and Compton.

RURAL SCENE AT HENDER'S CORNER

One could not be blamed for not recognising this spot at Mannamead. The road to the right goes to Compton, Efford and Eggbuckland and, to the left, to Tavistock. Car no. 9 is at the Compton terminus waiting to take passengers into Plymouth as far as the Theatre. The track up to this point was extended from Mutley Plain in April, 1893. The photograph is dated around 1910.

PASSING THE ST. LEVAN R.N. DOCKYARD GATE

Many trams served the Dockyard by bringing to the gates thousands of men and women over many years from various places roundabout. This photograph, of about 1910, shows one of the Devonport and District Tramway Company trams making its way to St. Budeaux. The route was working by June, 1901, up as far as Camel's Head. From here passengers had to walk across a long wooden bridge to reach two isolated trams working between Camel's Head and Saltash Passage.

TRAMWAY'S OFFICE IN EBRINGTON STREET

This moved from Market Street to 15 Ebrington Street in 1905 when re-organisation took place in the Plymouth Corporation Tramway Company. Car no. 24 is running along the first route to be electrified, Theatre to Prince Rock, which took place in 1899. The car was built in 1903 and was withdrawn from service by 1924. The track to Prince Rock was laid in 1896 and the company was founded in 1892.

TERMINUS AT ST. BUDEAUX

Tram no. 84, an ex-Devonport and District one, was in service from 1914 to 1930. Route 7 came into operation a little after 1903 when the embankment was built at Camel's Head. It was then possible to journey to St. Budeaux without having to change trams at Camel's Head. The Devonport and District Company started operating in 1901 using four and three-quarter miles of track over which 30 open top trams worked.

TORR LANE TERMINUS

This Devonport and District tram waits for passengers at the Torr Lane terminus. No. 8 tram was introduced in 1900 and ran until 1914 having been imported from America with nineteen others for this company. The D. and D. company had thirty-three trams in all which worked on the narrow 3 feet 6 inch track. From this terminus it was possible to travel to Devonport via Stoke or to Morice Square via St. Levan Road.

TURNING AT ST. ANDREWS CROSS IN 1920

This front end view of car no. 80, originally with the Devonport and District Company, makes the turn for the run to South Keyham. It was in service from 1914 until 1930 and shows the driver at the controls although exposed to the elements in a similar fashion to passengers sitting on the top deck. The route to South Keyham was no. 7 starting from the Guildhall, passing along Stuart Road and on eventually to St. Budeaux.

MORICE SQUARE TO ST. BUDEAUX SERVICE

Although the tram at the time of this photograph was part of the Plymouth Corporation Tramway fleet, the crest of the Devonport and District company can still be seen just under the route board. This service ran via Keyham using the narrow 3 feet 6 inch gauge track and the current came from the Devonport Corporation power station in Newport Street, Stonehouse.

FORE STREET, DEVONPORT

This scene in the very busy thoroughfare dates from about 1908 and shows car no. 9, of the Plymouth, Stonehouse and Devonport Tramways, which ran from 1901 to 1922. The companies' rolling stock comprised sixteen electric trams. After the amalgamation of Plymouth, Stonehouse and Devonport in 1914 the two distinct Devonport companies merged with the larger Plymouth company and many of their trams continued service with new numbers and colours.

OFF TO THE THEATRE

Is the well-dressed lady waiting to leave the tram going to the Theatre? Many of the Theatre's patrons must have reached this spot by tram from many parts of the Plymouth area during the early decades of this century. This car, no. 12, was introduced in 1900 and saw service until 1934. Here it is on the Peverell Park route and is further identified by a white metal circular disc fixed above the car no. Various trams had different coloured discs on them.

HUB OF THE TRAMWAY SYSTEM

This was at the Theatre close to Derry's clock and this typical scene shows a daily event of passengers getting off trams while other people are waiting to board them. Car no. 15, on the Theatre to Compton route, came into service in 1900 and was withdrawn by 1934. The rear tram is on the Theatre to Prince Rock service.

WAITING TO GO AT BEAUMONT ROAD TERMINUS

Car 24, on route 4, is ready to carry passengers to the Hoe and Piers when this photograph was taken in 1921. The Beaumont Road track was opened in April, 1902, and was later extended to Heathfield Road to serve the new council housing estates at Mount Gould. This tram ran from 1903 to 1924. The driver had at least some cover in bad weather by the upper deck canopy.

READY TO START FROM PRINCE ROCK

The Battery Cycle shop is still in business and this pin points the position of car no. 96 ready for its long route to Devonport via the places indicated on the window board. A telephone kiosk and public toilets formerly stood at this now busy junction some yards from the large Prince Rock School. This route had a red star painted on to a white circular metal plate to show people who could not read, the calling places of the tram.

MAINTENANCE WORK AT THE MILEHOUSE DEPOT

Although this depot was first built to service trams it was not long before coaches were included in its work. Today, of course, it serves the very large fleet of buses working in this area. This photograph was taken during the 1920s and shows car no. 42, working route 3, being checked while, on the right, two early coaches are in the depot for similar work.

TRAM CAR CONSTRUCTION AT MILEHOUSE

Although many of the trams were purchased from manufacturers, other tramway companies and some imported, local initiative was such that bodies were also built at Milehouse. This 1920s photograph shows carpenters at work putting together the large and heavily constructed wooden framework which would then be fixed onto bogies.

PLYMOUTH TRAMWAYS.

A CRITICISM.

The Report of the Electrical Engineer.

MANAGER'S REPLY.

MESSRS. OKELL AND EVERSON ON CARS AND EQUIPMENT.

The following are the report of the Electrical Engineer with regard to tram cars and overhead electrical equipment and the observations of the Tramways Manager thereon presented to the chairman and members of the Tramways Committee of the Plymouth Town Council.—

Prince Rock, August, 1907.

To the Chairman and Members of the Tramways Committee.

Gentlemen,—In accordance with the instructions contained in Minute numbered 2022 of the present year, I have the honour to submit the following report upon the Tramcars and Overhead Electrical Equipment of the Plymouth Tramways.

CARS.

The total number of electric cars is now 42; they have been purchased at different times and were brought into use as under, viz:—6 during the year 1899; 14 during the year 1901; 10 during the year 1902; 6 during the year 1906; 6 during the year 1907.

The number now in use for ordinary daily service is 27, leaving 15 for cars under repair, and cars for special service.

All the cars with the exception of those recently purchased show considerable signs of wear. This is no doubt due in some measure to the hilly and crooked nature of the routes traversed; also the rough state of the track tends to considerably increase the wear of the cars in operation.

Many of the truck attachments show signs of movement where bolted to the frames, the frames and packings being worn at the joints; a number of the bolts securing these parts together have been found slack.

A number of main axle springs have been broken, and in several instances I have found broken springs in place on cars in service.

It is undesirable to run a car under these conditions, as the vibration is increased, and there is risk of further injury.

I am of opinion that it would be desirable to try other forms and makes of these springs with a view to the adoption of a type better adapted to withstand the rough usage to which they are subjected.

The guide bolts of the truck springs are in some instances bent, impeding the action of the springs, and in several cases check washers are missing, allowing the bolts free play to rattle about, causing noise and wear.

Many of the bearings examined have been found to be considerably worn down, and in some the wear has been allowed to go too far, so that the bearing cases have been cut into, involving the replacement not only of the lining metal, but also of the casing castings. One or two bottom plugs are missing from oil wells under bearings, allowing the oil to escape.

The chains and rods of the brake gear are generally in sound condition, but rusty. A number of cotter pins holding connecting bolts in place are very loose and so much worn that they can be drawn out of place with the fingers, several are missing. In one instance I found the main bolt between the hand brake lever and connecting rod without nut or cotter pin, so that the bolt could be easily lifted out.

Several of the rods examined are a good deal worn at the joints and connections, and will require new ends at an early date; they are not lubricated in any way.

A number of the gear wheels are considerably worn down, and will soon require renewal. Several new ones were being fitted.

All nuts and bolts liable to work loose should be examined daily and tightened up where necessary; I have found many loose on different parts of the gear, all tending to increase the noise and wear.

COLLISION AT DEVONPORT

TRAMCAR AND MOTOR LORRY.

As the result of a collision between a tramcar and a motor lorry, the roadway near the R.N.E. College ground was yesterday strewn with bags of cabbages and potatoes.

The story of the accident is better told in the words of the driver of the lorry (Mr. H. Hocking) who, interviewed by one of our representatives said: "I was driving the lorry—a three tonner owned by Mr. J. C. Hawk and loaded with about three tons of cabbages and potatoes—towards St. Budeaux. I was rounding the corner by the College ground at about 5 miles per hour, when the tramcar ran into the rear of my lorry completely overturning it on its left side. I climbed over the top of the front hood and was not in the least hurt. The car was slightly damaged—the steering gear being broken by the impact. Mr. T. Hall, who was riding on the top of the load, was thrown to the ground, but fortunately escaped with little injury."

A glance at the tramcar showed that the front rails and supports were either broken or bent, while the whole of the glass on one side was completely smashed. Having regard to the fact that the car contained a fair complement of passengers, it is surprising that no one was cut by the falling glass. The tram service was delayed some time as the lorry and its contents lay across the outward line. Another motor lorry was fetched to tow away the damaged one.

TRAMWAY NEWS

There have been many newspaper reports on all aspects of the tramway system from notices of accidents to engineer's reports and how the system was coping with changes over the years. Two are shown here with part of the report authorising the development of a section of the Devonport and District services at the turn of the century. The wall plaque at Milehouse will be familiar to many people and it records the large depot facilities built in 1923.

The tramway authorised by this Order will be wholly situated within the borough and is as follows (that is to say) :—

A tramway (6 furlongs 5·70 chains in length) commencing by a junction with Tramway No. 8 authorised by the Devonport and District Tramways Act 1898 in Saltash Road at a point 0·80 chain or thereabouts west of the intersection of Wolseley Road and Saltash Road proceeding thence in a north-westerly direction along Saltash Road across Camel's Head Bridge thence in a westerly and thence in a north-westerly direction and terminating in Saltash Road at a point 1·74 chains west of Yeoman's Terrace Provided always that the tramway shall not be constructed upon Camel's Head Bridge until the bridge has been reconstructed and the carriageway thereof widened to thirty feet.

PLYMOUTH BUYS NINE TRAMS

BUT EXETER BIDS FAREWELL

"WONDERFUL FUNERAL ORATION"

Gaily beflagged and carrying civic representatives as passengers, the last tram to traverse the Exeter track passed out of active service yesterday, the driver being Mr. E. C. Perry, who, as Mayor, inaugurated the service by driving the first tram on April 4, 1905. The ceremony signified the passing of the tramway undertaking and the substitution of a complete municipal service of omnibuses.

Plymouth Corporation have purchased nine of the Exeter trams, seven at £150 each and two at £75 each. Four were previously sold to Halifax for £800, and the Council hope to find purchasers for the remaining thirteen. The cars disposed of have all been built since 1920.

The Mayor, who, with the Sheriff, members of the Council, and officials, was the guest of Mr. Bradley (chairman of the Transport Committee) at tea, served at the 'bus depot, wished success to the undertaking. "We have to progress," said his Worship. "Trams are an obstruction. It is no use saying they are not in face of the volume of traffic and the heavy and fast-moving vehicles of to-day. The Transport Committee realized they had to make a change, and in superseding the trams by 'buses they have done splendidly. The change-over has been effected with scarcely any inconvenience to anybody." So far as he could see the 'buses would be a huge success.

WALL JUNCTION BOX

This is still in position in the wall of Beaumont Park and was in use from 1899 when the Beaumont Road service was built. The letters "PC" and "EW" are on the metal door covering former electrical fittings inside. Two articles of 1931 and 1920 are shown and a pre-First World War view of the Guildhall and Bedford Street showing a tram starting off on the service to Devonport completes this page.

GROWING DEFICIT.

PLYMOUTH TRAM FIGURES DISAPPOINTING.

Sir Thomas Baker was yesterday elected chairman of the Plymouth Corporation Tramways Committee in accordance with the party arrangement already announced. —The Manager's (Mr. H. P. Stokes) monthly report, although not so grave as that presented to the October meeting, showed that the trams are still losing money, the receipts for the past four weeks amounting to £13,956, and the expenditure to £14,555, a deficiency of £599. The loss since March 31 last amounts to £12,000, approximately a threepenny rate. During the month 2,031,859 passengers were carried, and owing to the increased fares the receipts are £3,804 greater than they were last year. The average receipts per car mile have increased from 17.10d. to 22.59d.

The motor 'bus traffic shows a profit, the receipts to date being £2,605, and the expenditure £2,318. During the last four weeks the revenue was £1,307, and the expenditure £1,261. No allowance appears to be made in this latter figure for capital charges, the items comprising it being power expenses (£689), traffic expenses, wages (£351), cleaning and oiling (£62), repairs and maintenance (£61), road maintenance (£110), and miscellaneous (£4).

The Manager reported that the application from the Transport Workers' Federation for an increase of wages of 12s. per week to tramway employés over 18 years of age, and 6s. for youths under 18, had been considered by the National Joint Industrial Council, but no decision had been arrived at. A special meeting of the Municipal Tramways Association was being held next week to enable every tramway authority to express its views on this matter.—The committee appointed the chairman and the manager to attend the meeting.

With reference to the Tavistock-road and Wolseley-road (Devonport) improvement scheme, the Manager reported that the cost of converting the Tavistock-road track into a double track would be £33,698, while he estimated that it would cost £44,450 to extend the track along Wolseley-road.—This matter was deferred.

WAITING TO MOVE OFF

The driver, conductor and one bystander wait for more passengers at Prince Rock for the return journey into Plymouth. This is on route 5 which went through to Millbay via the main stop at the Theatre. The picture was taken about 1924 and by then trams had become the main method for Plymothians to get around their town. The fare structures were based upon a 1d. per stage up to 1914–18 then they went to 1½d. per stage.

FORE STREET, DEVONPORT, 1921

This Plymouth, Stonehouse and Devonport tram is waiting at the Fore Street stop for passengers wanting to journey to Plymouth. The car is a Dick Kerr and saw service from 1901 to 1922. It is on the route that was opened on 17th March, 1872, and for the first day only passengers could travel free! Trams had to cross the toll bridge at Stonehouse for which the company paid an annual premium until the tolls were lifted in 1924.

ENLARGED MILEHOUSE DEPOT

The much enlarged maintenance depot of the 1920s had cover for nine tracks along which a variety of work on trams could take place in the dry. Trams had many teething problems, extra brakes had to be fitted for steep hills, and others came in for modernising to increase passenger numbers. Two are seen here and, to the left, one coach is also in for what looks like repairs to its body work.

BASKET STREET TRACK LAYOUT

This view of the street and two trams shows the crossing points from track to track, the grooves of which were dangerous to cyclists whose wheels were known to get caught between the metals. The right hand car is on the well-known circular route 2. The new manager, Mr. C. Jackson, adopted a standard colour scheme in 1927 for trams. They were gold-lined marooned with cream-lined in red.

CHECKING ONE'S CHANGE

It looks like the passenger on the open upper deck is checking his change having paid his fare to the conductor who is returning to the lower deck. Car no. 1 is here on route 6 making its way to the Theatre. The place of this photograph has not been identified.

ON THE CIRCULAR ROUTE 2

This is given as *Theatre, Mutley, Peverell, Stoke* and *Union Street* which covered a good part of the town and enabled people to get off at any stage and pick up another tram further along the route. Here car no. 7 is passing Milehouse on its way to the Theatre although there are not many passengers in it. This could be due to most people being at work, as trams like buses today, had peak demands at the beginning and end of most days.

A CROWDED MILEHOUSE DEPOT

The dual role of servicing trams and buses is amply shown in this photograph taken in the early 1920s. Trams are in line for leaving on their various routes and many early buses similarly wait, the destination of a few indicated on them. Tram car no. 148 was in service from 1924 to 1938. The depot was rebuilt in 1923 then under the Plymouth Corporation Tramways.

ALL SET TO GO!

Tram no. 137 for route 3 is ready for service having just had an overhaul in the large Milehouse depot some time in the early 1930s. Known as a "square face", it was one of a new series of cars introduced in 1925. They all had been phased out of working by 1938. Route 3 ran from the Theatre to Morice Square via Mutley, Peverell, Milehouse and North Keyham.

AN EXTENDED CANOPY OVER THE CAB

This gives a good view of the modification that took place to many cars by extending the upper deck to the full length of the vehicle so enabling more passengers to be carried. Car no. 74 stands here at Milehouse depot after the extension and is ready to work route 6 which ran from the Guildhall to Fore Street, Devonport.

LOOKING EAST ALONG UNION STREET

This view of the busy thoroughfare was taken from the old railway bridge showing an approaching tram on route 12 heading for Fore Street, Devonport. It is in the early 1930s. The car has the covered in driver's cab and the upper deck runs the length of the vehicle. It probably started from the Guildhall or Theatre.

VIEW OF TRAM UPPER DECK

No protection for bad weather was allowed here although in some trams a protective sheet could be pulled over the passenger's legs. This picture was taken in Peverell Park Road and shows quite clearly the light fittings and the stanchion for the arm that collected the electric current from overhead wires.

ALL SET FOR SALTASH PASSAGE FROM THE HOE

Car no. 133, a "square face", was one of 24 delivered in the 1920s and saw service until 1939. The old horse-drawn car route to the Hoe was electrified in June, 1907, and was later linked with the network of the whole area. Route 14 was one of the longest in the area running from the Pier to Saltash Passage after 2 p.m. on summer days for a total of nine miles.

AN ALL TEAK TRAM

Tram no. 151 will be remembered with some affection as it was an experimental one introduced in 1925 and copied by later trams during the latter half of the 1920s. Designed and built by the Plymouth Corporation Tramways it saw service until 1945. The position of this photograph cannot be identified. The livery was varnished teak with gold linings and the shape of its front gave rise to them being called "square-faced" trams.

PASSING HOPE BAPTIST CHURCH, PEVERELL PARK ROAD

This very clear photograph shows an ex-Exeter Corporation tram purchased by the Plymouth Corporation in 1931 for £150. It served the Plymouth routes for about ten years and is seen here in about 1937 on the Peverell route which was opened in June, 1905. Notice the cobbled road surface which, in parts of the city, has been tarmacadamed over.

IN ALBERT ROAD, DEVONPORT

Car no. 8, a Brush tramcar, was purchased from the Exeter Corporation in 1931 and ran until 1937. Here it is on route 7 making its way from Devonport to the Theatre, Plymouth. This long-used route was extended to the Royal Naval Barracks so that navy personnel could easily reach Plymouth when on shore leave.

REFITTING AT THE MILEHOUSE DEPOT

It was very necessary from time to time not only to service tram cars but to modernise them to comply with new regulations or passenger loadings. Here one of the P.C.T. cars stands complete with its new external canopy extending over the driver's position so enabling more passengers to be carried than before. It is an ex-Devonport and District tram which was withdrawn by 1934.

Here it is sign-boarded for the route from the Theatre to Devonport, one of the most used lines in the area.

PASSING THE BRITANNIA INN AT MILEHOUSE

This still busy traffic junction was crossed by tracks of different routes and, of course, was very close to the main tramway's depot. The open upper deck gave a splendid view over the city as it passed from one end of a route to another. This is one of the "square-faced" trams and the picture comes from the latter half of the 1920s.

AWAITING PASSENGERS IN FORE STREET, DEVONPORT

This photograph of car no. 164 in 1936 shows it standing on the extensive circular route 2 in front of the once well-known Electric Cinema. The tram was one of a fleet introduced between 1926 and 1928 seeing service until 1942. This was one of the most patronised routes of the tramway system enabling passengers to alight at many stops between Devonport and the Theatre in Plymouth.

READY FOR DEPARTURE FROM DERRY'S CLOCK

These two cars were part of the new fleet introduced between 1926 and 1928 based upon the experimental 151 tram of 1925. Both saw service until the war years and the ending of the tramway system in Plymouth. Tram no. 156 looks like it is about to set out for Peverell while the other has just arrived at the Theatre stop. This building formerly stood to the immediate right of this photograph. On the left are waiting bays for passengers.

DESTINATION PRINCE ROCK

Electric tram car no. 12 stands in Chapel Street, Devonport, ready to start along one of the longest tramway routes in the area which was then route 12. This car was one of a fleet, numbered 7 to 20, which saw service from 1900 up until 1924.

TRAM SERVICES DURING THE BLITZ

The above photograph looks very much like it was taken after one of the many night raids on the city. The tramway overhead wires criss-cross this scene of great devastation at Perkens Corner, Bedford Street. The helmetted wardens are probably exhausted after a night's duty and the trams would certainly not be operating under the conditions shown here. Tidying up and street clearing has enabled some movement of people and traffic in the photograph below. The tram is moving towards Drake's Circus viewed from a little way up Old Town Street.

ALMOST GOODBYE TO PLYMOUTH'S TRAMS

This is 1945 and much of the centre of the city is tidied up after the devastation of the blitz which, of course, seriously affected the various tram services. Here car no. 158 crosses the now open city a few days before the final service. A makeshift terminus had been working in Old Town Street since the bombing and emergency repairs to rolling stock, tracks and the bombed Milehouse depot kept the system working for about another two years.

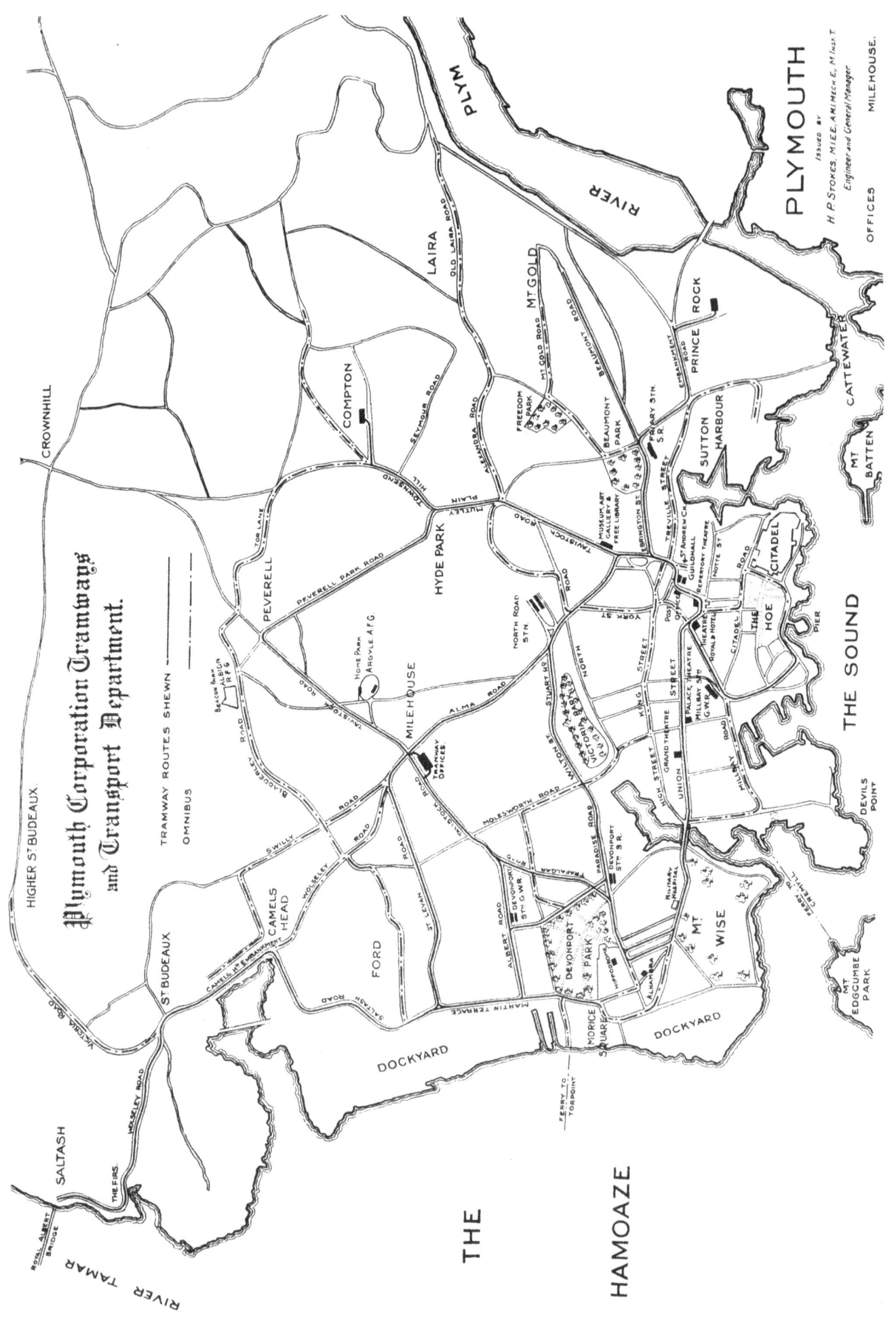

Arthur L. Clamp – the man behind the books

Arthur Leslie Clamp was a man of boundless energy with a passion for helping others, particularly through his love of history. A printer by trade, he started his career in a printing company before moving his family from Exeter to Plymouth to teach at the Plymouth College of Art and Design, where he eventually became the Head of the Printing Department.

Arthur with his five children.

A Devoted Family Man

Despite his love of teaching, Arthur prioritised his family, always making it home by 5:30pm for tea. He and his wife, Rosemary, raised five children: Susan, Angela, Elizabeth, David, and Steven. Arthur would often combine his love of family and history by taking his children on Sunday walks, encouraging them to appreciate historical monuments by taking photos or making crayon rubbings of gravestones for his books. The family home at 203 Elburton Road was a hub of activity, with a large garden, featuring a two-storey fort and a makeshift swimming pool.

A Lifelong Learner and Adventurer

Arthur's thirst for knowledge extended beyond history to a deep curiosity about the world. He was passionate about exploring different cultures, traditions, and cuisines, often taking advantage of his long summer holidays as a teacher to travel to places like India, Russia, South America, the middle east and the USA, sometimes bringing one of his children along. This adventurous spirit even influenced his home life, as seen by the short-lived family tradition of steam-cooking vegetables after a trip to Iceland.

History is a prominent feature of family days out

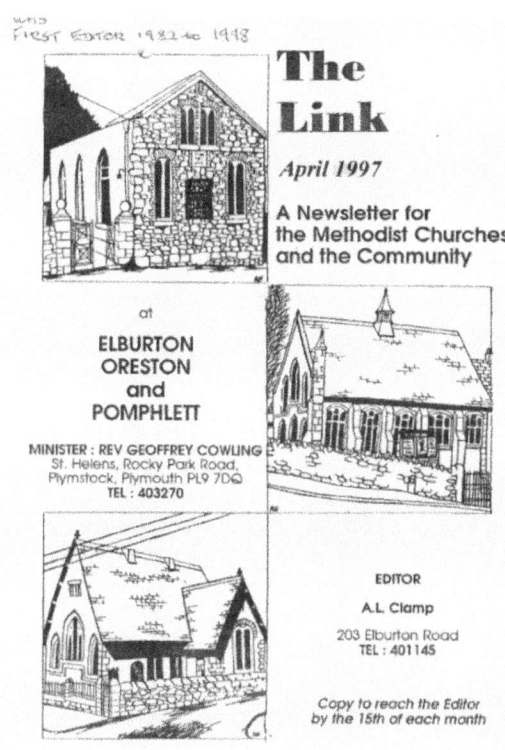

Community and Philanthropic Spirit

His commitment to serving others was evident in his long-standing involvement with the Elburton Methodist Church. He was the Sunday School Superintendent for over 15 years and served as the editor of the wider church's monthly newsletter, "The Link," for a similar duration. After Rosemary's very sad passing, Arthur later remarried and, following a chance encounter with a professor from India, established a connection with a missionary school in Chennai. Together with his new wife, Christine, he co-founded a "Sponsor a Child's Education" program that continues to this day.

Pictured left – The cover of 'The Link' complete with hand drawn sketches of each church by Angela
Below right – Arthur Clamp promoting his latest book
Below left – Arthur at home with his first wife, Rosemary
Below centre – Arthur on holiday with his second wife, Christine

A Legacy of Learning and Positivity

Arthur's greatest passion was history, which he brought to life through tireless research, documentation, and the many books he authored. He was driven by a need to "never be stuck in a rut," constantly seeking new experiences, meeting new people, and expanding his knowledge. With a positive attitude and a great sense of humour, he was always ready to help others, leaving a lasting impact on his family and community. His children, Susan, Angela, Elizabeth, David, and Steven, remember him with love and gratitude.

David Clamp, 2025

A Legacy of Local History

Below is the story of how Arthur L Clamp began writing books, in his own words, drafted shortly before he passed away in 2001. I have only made minor alterations to this text, correcting grammatical errors that he did not survive to correct himself. When I first discovered this text, I was shocked to see my name mentioned. It seems that, unbeknownst to me, I shared my first PC with him. I suspect he used it during the day when I was at school, although I do have one memory of sitting with him and showing him how it worked. It has been a pleasure to pick up where he left off and see his books republished and redistributed, and to know that I was part of the story, even back then. It was also fascinating to discover that his pricing structure matches the way I have tried to price the books, with a third going to local sellers and the rest covering printing costs with a little left over for my expenses.

I am his eldest grandson, and it is a privilege to curate his legacy, which we are calling 'The Clamp Collection'. The very last line of the text originally reads "The following pages list all the titles." Sadly, that page is missing and we have no record of all the books he published and knowing that some of those were researched by other authors makes the process of finding them even harder. I look forward to one day completing the collection and seeing them all available again. And maybe, one day, I'll even start writing my own to add to the series. For now, here is his story in his own words.

Steven Gibson, 2025

Writing and Publishing Booklets on Local Topics and Areas

I started this interest in either 1968 or 1969 when living in Woodford. I had by these dates established the Department of Printing and I think I must have been looking for something different to do. The first titles were of A5 size proofed from type set at Clarke, Doble and Brendon, Ltd., Plymouth printers, and then made up into pages and printed at Sawtell and Neilson, Ltd., Totnes.

Then began a slow process of getting them out to shops, etc. which proved to be more time consuming and difficult than actually researching, writing and getting the books into print. However, I persisted and opened a business account with Barclays Bank on the Broadway. I was advised to give it a title so I called it "Westway Publications". There came along another problem, one of storage of paper and finished books which was solved when the family moved to Elburton in 1970.

I changed the printer to Penwell, Ltd., Callington, Cornwall, as he was then just setting up himself and his prices seemed very reasonable. I did not get any of the printers to make up the complete books. I hand folded the flat printed sheets, stitched the books on a small manual table stitcher and trimmed them in a small hand turned guillotine which I bought from someone in Penzance for £40. It was brought up in a van.

The trouble and time going to and fro to Callington was too much so I transferred the printing to PDS Printers, Prince Rock, Plymouth, and I have been with them ever since. Now they are at Plympton which is easy to reach and they fold the flat sheets which was turning out to be a long chore which only saved a small part of the printing costs.

All my first titles were written by myself. I took the photographs and developed them in the loft of the house, the type was set by now on a computer situated in the house at Elburton from which I had collected photographic lengths of text to cut up and law down as pages.

At some point I decided that I would do my own film processing of lith film so I bought a large second hand process camera from Kingsbridge and learnt through trial and error to make line negatives of the text and halftone negatives of the illustrations which proved more difficult than I anticipated. The main problem was trying to keep the developer in the large dish at the correct temperature as any change would affect the developing time. I replaced this old camera with a brand new one bought from Croydon, Surrey, costing £900. This has turned out to be a great asset cutting out an expensive part of the printer's costs and one crucial aspect of the work which I could control.

By the middle 1970s there were many outlets I had contacted in Plymouth, up to Dartmoor, Exeter, around to Torbay, Totnes, Dartmouth and the South Hams. The market for local books was much greater than I had first thought and through getting to know many local people undertaking research themselves had the chance to help and make up books for other people who had in most instances, got together a collection of photographs with some text in a rather muddled way. Through my experience in print I was able to shape up their work and get it into print and in every case I had to pay the printer and let the person have the royalties. In the majority of titles produced in this manner this was another way of producing titles and it did give some profit to my work. However, I must say that in a few cases I lost out by either the other person getting the numbers wrong, not returning any monies from stock I delivered or they thought that more of their books should have been sold.

The print run was usually 1,000 copies and from time to time I have had reprints of 250 copies. It took about ten years to clear the first print run so I always had large stocks in the garage, workshop, etc. The numbers sold during the early years was about 7,000 copies a year increasing to around 9,000 copies and for the whole of the enterprise about 500,000 have been sold. The booklets have become part of the local scene and many people collect them, shops regularly order copies and I go around certain areas month by month restocking or replacing titles as necessary.

During the past year or so I have started setting the text on a Packard Bell PC, something which I should have done some years back. I share it with Steven Gibson, my grandson. There appears to be no end to the market for local books, but I could not earn a regular income because of the long time it takes to sell stock.

However, now exceeding 100 titles made up mainly of A4 twenty-four page booklets, some folded guides, with selling prices set with a third going to the shop which is the trade custom, the original idea has been quite successful and could go on for ever.

Apart from monetary benefits, however spasmodically these might be, I have learnt a lot myself, met many interesting people and have become part of the local scene with requests to give talks and to advise people about getting into print.

Arthur L Clamp, 2001

This newspaper article, published by the Evening Herald on 17th August 2001, forms a good record of his life. Just as he encourages us to learn more about local history, we encourage you to learn a little about him. For that reason, we have included these pages at the back of all the most recently republished books, in honour of his memory and recognition of his contribution to the community.